Paraphrases and Questions for 25 Psalms

Psalms for Kids

Robert Baden

Illustrated by Michelle Dorenkamp

CONCORDIA PUBLISHING HOUSE • SAINT LOUIS

Text copyright © 2001 Robert Baden

Illustrations copyright © 2001 Concordia Publishing House

Published by Concordia Publishing House

3558 S. Jefferson Avenue, St. Louis, MO 63118-3968

Manufactured in the United States of America

	3	4	5	6	7	8	9	10	11
13	12	11	10	09	08	07	06	05	

Contents

Dedication

*This book is dedicated
in memory of the author,
Robert Baden,
whose faith and life
touched many of God's children—
both young and old.*

Psalm 1

The happy person is the one
Who chooses not to walk
With those who treasure evil things
Or laugh at sinful talk.
The happy person loves to read
And follow God's commands,
Like fruit-filled trees on fertile ground,
This person firmly stands.
The wicked people aren't like this;
Their lives are sad and dry.
Like worthless weeds, they soon turn brown;
They shrivel up and die.
God blesses those with peace and joy
Who walk His wiser way.
And when they die, He'll take them home
On His great Judgment Day.

1. What does the psalm say makes a person truly happy?

2. What does the psalm suggest about who our friends should be?

3. The psalm compares people to plants. What differences do you see? What is the same?

Prayer:

Dear God, help me choose friends who do the kinds of things that would please You. And when I lead, help me walk in ways that will not lead others into evil places. In Jesus' name. Amen.

Psalm 3

O Lord, so many threaten me
And fill me with alarm.
They laugh at me and say that You
Can't keep me from their harm.
But I know You're my shield, O Lord,
You guard and keep me still.
When I cry out for help, You come
Down from Your holy hill.
I fall asleep with You each night
And wake secure from harm.
I will not fear though thousands try
To tear me from Your arms.
Come quickly, Lord, deliver me,
My enemies draw near.
Crush all who now endanger me,
Who try to make me fear.
For You alone can guard me, Lord,
Joy only comes from You.
You guard and keep me every day
And bless all that I do.

1. What is one thing that makes you feel afraid?

2. What do you usually do when you are frightened?

3. What does the psalm suggest we should do when we feel afraid?

Prayer:

Dear Lord, help me to remember to talk to You when I'm afraid. Help me trust in Your protection at all times. For Jesus' sake. Amen.

Psalm 8

O mighty, great, and glorious God,
Your name I gladly praise.
You punish sin, but those who trust,
You bless for all their days.
When I look up into the sky
Your moon and stars to see,
I wonder why You'd take the time
To notice one like me.
But then You say You've made me king
Of all of Your creation.
You gave me wisdom, beauty, strength,
And promised me salvation.
You've made me ruler over all
The things that I can see:
The birds and animals and all
That travel through the sea.
So when I see Your awesome world,
My thankful voice I raise:
O mighty, great, and glorious God,
Your name I gladly praise!

1. What do you think is the most beautiful thing in the world?

2. How are people different from other things in nature?

3. Why does God take the time to notice each one of us?

Prayer:

Dear Lord, thank You for our wonderful world. Help us to praise You for its beauty each day of our lives. In Jesus' name. Amen.

Psalm 19

The heavens show Your glories, God,

The skies shout out your might.

Without a voice, they still can share

Your power and their delight.

The sun comes forth at Your command

And warms the world You've made.

It circles all around the earth

And shines away the shade.

Your laws of nature and of life

Are worth far more than gold.

They give me wisdom, bring me joy,

Will comfort when I'm old.

You promise great reward as I

Obey what You have spoken.

Keep me, O Lord, from every sin,

Forgive the rules I've broken.

May what I speak and think, O Lord,

Be pleasing in Your sight.

You are my Rock and Savior, Lord,

My Strength both day and night.

1. How do laws of nature help us be wise or bring us joy and comfort?

2. What do these laws of nature tell us about God?

3. What is one thing we can do to take care of God's world?

Prayer:

Dear Lord, help us find delight in this world You have given us, and to take good care of it. For Jesus' sake. Amen.

Psalm 23

My Shepherd is the Lord Himself
And I'm His little lamb.
With all the people in the world,
He still knows who I am.
He meets my daily needs and then
Leads me to pastures green.
There He restores my thirsty soul
With waters fresh and clean.
He knows both good and evil paths
Stretched out for me to use.
He teaches me so I will know
The one I ought to choose.
And when through danger I must pass,
My Shepherd walks there too,
To guard and keep me safe from harm
And bless all that I do.
When evil people gather near
And threaten me with ill,
My Lord prepares a feast of love
Where I can eat my fill.
He pours His mercies over me,

His goodness never slows.
I don't deserve it, but my cup
Of blessing overflows.
His kindness in the past makes clear
More goodness lies in store.
And when I die, I know I'll live
With Him forevermore.

1. How does it make you feel to realize that God knows who you are?

2. How are we like sheep? Why do we need a Shepherd?

3. Why is the writer so sure that God will always be with him?

Prayer:

Dear Good Shepherd, I know I often stray off the path and get lost. Please come and find me when that happens and keep me close to You always. In Your name I pray. Amen.

Psalm 27

The Lord's my Savior and my light,
I have no need to fear.
He fills my feeble life with strength,
And He is always near.
When enemies try to attack,
I will not be afraid;
Not even mighty armies will
Be able to invade.
To live inside His holy house
Is all I ask my Lord;
To see His beauty every day,
To feel His love outpoured.
I know I'll live in safety there,
My life will be secure;
And there I'll worship Him with joy,
With music sweet and pure.
I know He'll hear me when I call,
That He will never leave;
Though other people turn away,
His servant He'll receive.
In times of trouble I'll take heart,

I'll wait and still be strong.
I know I'll see His goodness soon;
My wait will not be long.

1. What enemies do you have who threaten your faith?

2. Why do you think the writer says that we can feel safe and secure when we worship in God's holy house?

3. How can you know that God will help you, even if it's not right away?

Prayer:

Dear God, whenever I feel danger and temptation, be close to me and protect me with Your almighty power. Make me strong to do Your will. In Jesus' name. Amen.

Psalm 29

All strength and glory are the Lord's;
Give honor to His name.
And praise His splendid holiness,
That always is the same.
His voice is louder than the waves,
It echoes like the thunder;
It rings with power and majesty
And fills our hearts with wonder.
Like lightning strikes the trees, His voice
Comes flashing from the sky.
And "Glory to our mighty Lord!"
All in His temple cry.
The Lord sits high above the seas,
Our mighty, heavenly King.
He blesses us with strength and peace,
No wonder that we sing!

1. Can you think of someone in Bible times who actually heard the voice of God?

2. Does God ever speak to us? When and how?

3. If God spoke to you today, what do you think He might say?

Prayer:

Dear Lord, thank You for the special gift of your Your words in the Bible and the people who teach them to me. Help me listen to what You say to me. For Jesus' sake. Amen.

Psalm 33

All those who truly love the Lord,

Sing out and praise His name.

Compose new songs for harp and strings,

Sing praises to His name.

His Word is always right and true

On earth and heav'n above.

His perfect justice gently flows

Down on us with His love.

He spoke and stars knew where to go,

And shores held back the sea.

We praise His name, for when He spoke,

Creation came to be.

Kings in their foolishness believed

Their little plans were grand;

The Lord destroyed theirs with a breath

While His forever stand.

The only nations sure to last

Are those that serve the Lord.

All those who trust in their own strength

Will gain their sad reward.

No mighty army is enough

To change a single thing;
No warrior's strength, no mighty horse
Can help an evil king.
But those who trust upon the Lord,
Who treasure most His love,
Who hope in Him, their help and shield,
Will find reward above.

1. What do you see happening to show that our nation is serving the Lord?

2. What things show that our nation does not always serve the Lord?

3. Why should we care what the leaders of our nation do?

Prayer:

Dear Lord, bless the leaders of our nation and help them do Your will. Help us remember that You are more powerful than any nation on earth. In Jesus' name. Amen.

Psalm 34

Each day I celebrate the Lord
And praise Him with my voice.
Let all who suffer join with me
And soon they will rejoice.
Let all in danger hear my words
And call upon His name;
Their faces soon will shine like stars,
Completely free from shame.
The angel of the Lord stands near
All those who love the Lord;
From danger He delivers them,
On them His love is poured.
Much blessed are those who trust the Lord,
He meets their every need;
Though lions have no food to eat,
His children He will feed.
The key to long and fruitful lives
Is simple, plain, and true:
Keep far away from evil things,
Good things and peace pursue.
The Lord hears when His children cry

And takes their griefs away.
But those whose lives are filled with sin
Are lost and left to stray.
The children of the Lord must face
Life's pains and troubles too;
But He will see their needs and come
To heal and make them new.

1. What should we do when we are troubled?

2. If people suffer, does it mean God is angry and is punishing them?

3. What is meant when the writer says "their faces will shine like stars?"

Prayer:

Dear Lord, when we are sick or in danger, remind us to look to You for help and protection. And help us look forward to that day when our faces will shine like stars for Jesus' sake. In His name I pray. Amen.

Psalm 42

Like thirsty deer long for a drink,
I long for You, O Lord.
My soul is parched, I'm filled with tears,
I'm lost and feel ignored.
So many laugh and say to me,
"Where is this Lord you praise?"
I think of how You seemed so near
Back in far better days.
I try to keep from being sad,
Remembering Your love.
On You I still place all my hope
And look for help above.
It seems that You've forgotten me
And I'm so tired and lost;
I'm like a little boat at sea,
By angry waters tossed.
Just when I'm at the lowest point,
I sense that You are near.
In You I hope, I'll praise You still,
My Lord and Savior dear.

1. Do Christians ever feel lost and forgotten? When and why?

2. Can you think of anyone in the Bible who felt God was far away and didn't care?

3. What does the writer say we can we do if we feel lost or long for the Lord?

Prayer:

Dear Lord, whenever I feel sad, tired, lost, or forgotten, please remind me that You love me and that You are near. For Jesus' sake. Amen.

Psalm 46

God is our strength and hiding place
Whenever troubles rise.
We have no need to be afraid
Wherever danger lies.
Although the whole earth breaks apart,
And mighty mountains fall;
Though earthquakes shake and oceans roar,
He's Master of them all.
God lives where rivers softly flow,
Where peace and safety stay;
Though war is raging all around,
He melts our fears away.
Our God Himself is guarding us
With His almighty arms.
Just like a castle on a hill,
He keeps us safe from harm.
Look 'round and see how He's destroyed
All evil in the land;
The weapons used for making war
Lie broken in the sand.
He speaks to us with power and love:

"Be still and know My worth;
I am your God, far stronger than
The nations of the earth."
Yes, God Himself is guarding us
With His almighty arm;
Just like a castle on a hill,
He keeps us from all harm!

1. How can we know God is stronger than anything and anyone on the earth?

2. What can we remember when things that seem bad happen?

3. Why don't we need to be afraid when terrible things happen?

Prayer:

Dear God, we thank You for giving us comfort and courage when we face danger. Please be with us in all times of trouble. In Jesus' name. Amen.

Psalm 51

Have mercy on me, mighty God,
I long to feel Your love.
I've sinned and beg You to forgive
What I am guilty of.
My sin is always on my mind,
It haunts me night and day.
I knew it wasn't right, but still
I did it anyway.
Not only those I sin against
Are hurt by what I do,
The sinful actions of my life
Are felt, O God, by You.

I've been a sinner all my life,
This awful truth I know.
Please wash away these sinful stains
And make me white as snow.
Instead of feeling guilt and fear,
Let me know joy at last.
Instead of seeing what I've done,
Forget my sinful past!
Make pure my sinful heart, O God,
Renew my sickened soul.
Don't throw me out into the dark,
Restore me, make me whole!

Then I will share Your love with all,
And they will seek You too.
Save me and I will sing new songs
To praise and honor You.
My lips will now declare Your praise,
And as my sacrifice—
I'll bring to You a broken heart;
I pray You won't despise.
And when my heart and soul are clean,
In thankfulness I'll bring
A life of service, love, and joy,
That's fitting for my King.

1. What are we to do when we know
we have sinned?

2. How does it hurt God when we hurt
other people?

3. What did Jesus do so that we might
receive forgiveness for our sins?

Prayer:

Dear Lord, be merciful to me, a sinner.
I ask not only that You forgive what I have
done wrong, but that You help me follow
Your will to do what is right. I know I can't
do that without Your help. Thank You for
sending Jesus to take my sins to the cross.
In His name I pray. Amen.

Psalm 65

We praise You, great and mighty God,
We bring You thanks today.
When we were overwhelmed by sins,
You took them all away.
We know You hear our every prayer,
To You all people come.
You answer us with awesome deeds
And make Your house our home.
You formed the mountains with Your might,
You calmed the roaring sea.
All near and far can see Your power,
Wherever they might be.
You touch our land with tender care,
You send forth timely rain;
And in the fall our carts are filled
And overflow with grain.
The meadows are alive with sheep,
The hillsides bloom each spring.
And even deserts grow with grass;
We shout for joy and sing!

1. What are three examples of God's blessings in this psalm?

2. What are three examples of God's blessings in your own life?

3. How might we respond to God who blesses us so richly?

Prayer:

Dear Lord, we praise You with a thankful heart for all that You have done for us, especially for sending Jesus as our Savior. Give us strong voices to sing Your praise! For Jesus' sake. Amen.

Psalm 84

O Lord, how lovely is the place
That you have made Your home.
My fainting soul longs for Your courts,
No longer left to roam.
The swallow leaves the wilds to nest
In safety near Your throne.
All those who dwell with You are blessed
And praise Your name alone.
And blessed are those who use Your strength
When they must leave Your land—
Fresh water fills their desert paths
And cools the burning sand.
Please hear my prayer, almighty God,
Please listen when I call.
Look down on me with favor now
As at Your feet I fall.
One day spent here within Your house
Is so much better, Lord,
Than thousands wasted somewhere else;
You are my great reward.
I'd rather humbly open doors

And be Your servant here
Than live with riches in a land
Where wickedness is near.
You are my Sun and Shield, O Lord,
You honor me with fame.
You hold back nothing that is good
From all who bless Your name.

1. What do you think the writer means when he talks about "God's house?"

2. Why does the writer of this psalm find peace and joy in God's house?

3. What can you do to honor the house of God?

Prayer:

Dear God, please help me always remember to keep Your house a holy place in all I do or say. In Jesus' name. Amen.

Psalm 90

Lord, You have been a home to us

Since time and life began;

Before creation, You set forth

Your everlasting plan.

A thousand years are but a glance

In Your eternal sight;

They're but a minute of the day,

A portion of the night.

All men and women come and go

As passing as a sigh—

Each morning they appear like grass,

By eveningtime they die.

Most lives last eighty years or less,

And trouble fills each day.

We sadly watch the years race past,

Until we die someday.

Have mercy on Your people, Lord,

Please hear us when we pray.

Show us Your love; we'll sing for joy

And celebrate each day.

Send years of happiness to match

The pain that we've gone through.
Let all who serve You see Your love
And bless the work they do.

1. If our lives pass so quickly, do you think they are still important to God?

2. What is the difference between God's time and our time?

3. What can you do to celebrate each day?

Prayer:

Dear God, even when we seem to have problems and much sadness, show us Your love and help us celebrate each day. For Jesus' sake. Amen.

Psalm 95

Come, sing with gladness to the Lord,

The Rock of our salvation.

Come, praise Him now with songs of thanks,

Great Ruler of our nation.

For He is King above all else,

The greatest One of all—

He rules the depths beneath the earth,

Tall hills obey His call.

He owns the sea because He placed

The waters where they flow.

He used His hands to shape the earth

And caused all life to grow.

Come worship, bow before the Lord.

Come kneel before our King.

He's our Good Shepherd, we're His flock;

We owe Him everything!

1. Why is it comforting to know God is the "Rock" of our salvation?

2. As Creator, what power does God have over everything He has made?

3. Why is it important that the Almighty God is also our "Good Shepherd?"

Prayer:

Dear God, help us remember that You have power over everything in our world. Help us also remember Your gentleness as our Loving Shepherd. In Jesus' name. Amen.

Psalm 96

Come sing a new song to the Lord!
Proclaim His great salvation!
Tell once again His glorious deeds
To each and every nation.
The Lord alone deserves our praise,
Come quickly and adore Him.
All other gods are make-believe;
They cannot stand before Him.
The Lord created earth and sky.
He reigns alone in splendor.
He moves in majesty and strength,
Our glorious Defender.
All nations, come before the Lord
And praise His strength and glory.
Give Him the honor He deserves
And tell the world His story!
Bow down and worship in His courts,
Bring offerings of love.
His judgments are both firm and fair
On earth and heaven above.
The heav'ns rejoice, the earth is glad,

The roaring oceans pound.
The joyful fields will celebrate,
And trees with joy resound.
All life will sing before the Lord
Who comes to judge the land.
He'll judge with fairness and with truth
That all will understand.

1. Other than praising God, what else can our songs do?

2. How can we tell that other gods are not like the One True God?

3. Where do we go to worship God in His courts?

Prayer:

Dear God, help us always remember that there are no other gods before You and that Your love and mercy endure forever. Lead us to worship You and come into Your house with thanksgiving. For Jesus' sake. Amen.

Psalm 98

The Lord has done amazing things,
Come sing new songs of praise!
He's won salvation by His might,
And blessed us all our days.
The Lord has kept His promises
To those He calls His own.
The nations all have seen the love
And goodness He has shown.
So, earth, rejoice! Shout out your joy!
Pour forth your joyful songs!
Use harp and horn and trumpet sound,
All praise to Him belongs!
All living in the sea, make noise!
Rejoice, all life on earth!
Come, rivers, loudly clap your hands,
And mountains, sing with mirth!
Let all sing praises to the Lord
Who comes to judge the land.
He'll judge with justice fairly poured
From His forgiving hands.

1. What promises has God kept in your life?

2. What blessings do you feel like shouting about?

3. What things in nature teach you about God and help you feel close to Him?

Prayer:

Dear God, remind me to look around in my life and see all the good You have given to me—especially Your love and forgiveness through Jesus. Then help me shout it to the world. In Jesus' name. Amen.

Psalm 103

My soul and body, praise the Lord!

Yes, praise His holy name!

Remember all the good He's done,

His holiness proclaim!

It's He that pardons all our sins

And heals disease and pain.

He feels compassion when we're sad

And cheers us up again.

The things our heart desires most

Our Lord most surely brings.

When we feel weak, He gives us strength

To soar on eagle's wings.

He's filled with sympathy and love,
Forgiving every sin.
As we repent, He gives us strength—
Renews our hearts within.
His love's as great as heaven is far
Above the earth below;
He's sent our sins so far away
That they no longer show.
Just as a father loves his child,
The Lord loves each of us;
He knows that at creation's hour,
He made us out of dust.

He knows that we are like the grass
That lives for just a day,
Before we wither in the wind
And quickly fade away.
But from time's start until its end,
The Lord still loves the same;
He blesses all who keep His Law
And glorify His name.
Praise Him, you saints and angel hosts!
Praise Him, who do His will!
Praise Him, all creatures in the world!
And I, too, praise Him still!

1. What does it mean that God gives us strength to soar on eagle's wings?

2. Why is it important that we repent and trust in God for forgiveness?

3. How is God's love like a parent's love?

Prayer:

Dear God, thank You for forgiving us and help us to be truly sorry for our sins. Lift us up on eagle's wings and give us strength to do Your will. For Jesus' sake. Amen.

Psalm 113

Praise Him, all servants of the Lord,

Come praise His holy name!

O let His mighty name be praised,

Forevermore the same!

From where the morning sun comes forth

To where it disappears,

His deeds and wonders can be known

By everyone who hears.

The Lord is higher than the skies,

And greater than all kings.

His holy name should be proclaimed

By everyone who sings.

For who is like the Lord, our God?

His throne is placed so high

That He must stoop to even look

Down on the earth and sky.

He lifts the needy from the dirt,

The poor from garbage piles.

He seats them with the Prince Himself

And fills their lives with smiles.

To those without a single child

To be the parents of,

He sends them sons and daughters too,

And fills their homes with love.

So praise the Lord! Yes, praise the Lord

For all that He has done;

Then go to all the world and tell

This news to everyone!

1. What are your favorite songs to praise the might and majesty of God?

2. Can you name some of the people that others might ignore, but God still blesses?

3. Since we know the wonderful things that God has done, what are we to do with that news?

Prayer:

Dear God, help us see and appreciate all the blessings You pour on us. Open our lips to praise You and tell everyone what You have done! In Jesus' name. Amen.

Psalm 121

You look up to the hills for help,
But that's of little worth;
Your help comes only from the Lord
Who made both heav'n and earth.
He will not let you slip and fall,
He never falls asleep.
He promises to keep you safe—
His promises He'll keep.
The Lord keeps watching over you;
You will not come to harm.
He'll shade you from the noonday sun
And from the night's alarm.
The Lord will keep you from all harm
Throughout your earthly ways.
He'll guard you as you come and go
Both now and all your days.

1. What are some of the wrong places that people look for God?

2. Why can you sleep and live your life without worry?

3. Where and when do you especially need the protection of God?

Prayer:

Dear God, since You are awake all the time and looking out for us, put all our worries to rest and keep us safely in the palm of Your hand. For Jesus' sake. Amen.

Psalm 130

From depths of pain, I call you, Lord.

O Lord, please hear my voice,

For You alone are merciful,

I have no other choice.

If You kept track of all our sins,

Who, Lord, could even stand?

But You have promised to forgive;

Somehow You understand.

My soul waits faithfully for You,

I know what You can do.

Like watchmen wait for morning's light,

My spirit waits for You.

Come, put your hope in God, the Lord,

In Him true love begins.

Just as He's cancelled others' faults,

He'll wash away your sins.

1. Write a list of your sins, whisper it to God, then throw the list away.

2. How is the coming of the morning like God coming to bless us?

3. Why is the forgiveness of our sins such a valuable blessing?

Prayer:

Dear God, we know we sin every day. Thank You for sending Jesus to take our sins to the cross. Please forgive us, and help us walk the path You choose for us, forgiving those who sin against us. In Jesus' name. Amen.

Psalm 146

Sing out, my soul, and praise the Lord,
Come fill the earth with praise;
I'll gladly sing my praise to God
However long my days.
Don't place your trust in human hands
Who try but cannot save;
They, just like you, will one day die
And join you in the grave.
The truly blessed hope in the Lord;
They know what He can do;
For He made earth and sky and sea
And all that lives there too.
The Lord is faithful to His Word;
He sets the prisoner free,
He feeds the poor, defends the wronged,
And makes the blind to see.
The Lord hears those who seek His help
And guards those most alone;
He crushes wickedness and rules
Forever on His throne.

1. Why can't other people save us from danger and death without God's help?

2. Why is God able to do what people cannot do?

3. How can we also be God's servants to those who have so little in life?

Prayer:

Dear God, help me trust in You above all others. Give me the words and courage to tell others how much I trust You. For Jesus' sake. Amen.

Psalm 148

All life and nature, praise the Lord!

All angels, praise the One!

And praise Him, all in endless space,

The moon and stars and sun!

For everything that is, He made

By His almighty power.

And what He made won't disappear

Until earth's final hour.

Praise Him, all creatures of the earth,

Sea creatures large and small!

Come, lightning, hail, dark clouds, and snow,

Come, praise Him, one and all!

Come, mountains, hills, fruit trees, and firs,

Come, creatures wild and tame,

Come, birds and creatures of all kinds

And praise His holy name!

Come, kings and princes of each land,

Come, all on earth who live,

Come, men and women, boys and girls,

Come and your praises give!

Together let us praise the Lord,

Who's called us as His own.

His glory shines beyond the earth,

All praise is His alone!

1. How do you think animals and nonliving things in nature praise God?

2. If animals and nature bring honor and glory to God, how should we treat them?

3. What are some of the things you praise God for?

Prayer:

Dear Father, make us aware of all the wonderful things in Your creation and teach us how to take proper care of them. In Jesus' name. Amen.

Psalm 150

Praise God inside His holy place,

Praise Him in heaven above!

Praise Him for all His mighty works

And His unending love.

Praise Him with trumpets' mighty sound!

Praise Him with harp and lyre!

Praise Him with tambourine and dance!

He fills our heart's desire!

Praise Him with singing, strings, and flute!

Clang cymbals loud and long!

With joyful noises, praise the Lord,

Make each a holy song!

Let everything with life and breath,

Pause now and praise the Lord.

Let all of nature join its voice

In one harmonious chord!

1. When and where are we to praise the Lord? What do you praise Him for?

2. Is loud music all right to use in church? When?

3. This is the last psalm in the Bible. Why is it so fitting to be the last?

Prayer:

Dear God, help us praise You for Your love and forgiveness with our whole body and soul, using old and new songs, loud and soft songs, and even silent songs in our heart. For Jesus' sake. Amen.